George W. BUSH

Herón Márquez

Lerner Publications Company
Minneapolis

With great love and admiration to my wife, Traecy, whose soaring spirit is matched only by her beauty and her sense of humor.

This book is available in two bindings:
Library binding by Lerner Publications Company,
  a division of Lerner Publishing Group
Soft cover by First Avenue Editions,
  an imprint of Lerner Publishing Group
241 First Avenue North
Minneapolis, MN 55401 U.S.A.

Website address: www.lernerbooks.com

Library of Congress Cataloging-in-Publication Data

Márquez, Herón.
    George W. Bush / by Herón Márquez.
      p.   cm. — (A&E biography)
    Includes bibliographical references and index.
    ISBN: 0-8225-4995-6 (lib. bdg. : alk. paper)
    ISBN: 0-8225-5001-6 (pbk. : alk. paper)
    1. Bush, George W. (George Walker), 1946—Juvenile literature.
    2. Presidents—United States—Biography—Juvenile literature.
    3. Governors—Texas—Biography—Juvenile literature. 4. Businessmen—
Texas—Biography—Juvenile literature. 5. Children of presidents—
United States—Biography—Juvenile literature. I. Title. II. Biography
(Lerner Publications Company)
E903.M37 2002
973.931'092—dc21   2001002017

Manufactured in the United States of America
1 2 3 4 5 6 – JR – 07 06 05 04 03 02

CONTENTS

George W. Bush overcame many personal and political obstacles on his journey to the presidency.

INTRODUCTION

Despite being born into one of the wealthiest and most powerful families in the country, success early in life never came easy for George Walker Bush. He did not do well in school, was defeated in his first political race, failed at early business ventures, battled a drinking problem, and endured countless jokes and questions about his intellectual ability. Yet he had the last laugh when he was sworn in as the forty-third president of the United States on January 20, 2001. His road to the White House was, however, far from smooth.

From the beginning, Bush faced a serious challenge from within his own Republican Party. Senator John McCain, a Vietnam War hero, defeated Bush in the first presidential primary election of 2000. Even after Bush managed to win his party's nomination for president, fellow Republicans questioned the way he ran his campaign against the Democratic challenger, Vice President Al Gore. Although Bush finally prevailed over Gore, he lost the popular vote in what was probably the most disputed presidential election in American history.

When Americans went to bed on November 7, 2000, few could have imagined the election results would be hotly debated for the next five weeks. The controversy caught the attention of the world as legal and political fights broke out over the outcome of the election in Florida, where Bush's younger brother Jeb was governor.

SOME ELECTORAL HISTORY

s wild, dramatic, and nerve-racking as the 2000 presidential election was for the country and the world, it was not unique in U.S. history. In fact, the race between George W. Bush and Al Gore was the fifth time that a candidate had become president by losing the popular vote and winning the electoral vote.

The first time it happened was in 1800, when it took several days and thirty-six ballots in the House of Representatives for Thomas Jefferson to be selected president over Aaron Burr. The two candidates had a tie vote in the electoral college with seventy-three votes each from the nineteen states in the Union at that time. The result was seventy-three electors voting for Jefferson and seventy-three voting for Burr. Since there was no clear winner in the electoral college, election rules required that the matter be turned over to the House of Representatives to determine the next president. The vote finally swung in Jefferson's favor when Alexander Hamilton, who hated Burr, convinced enough representatives to vote for Jefferson. Burr, who never forgave Hamilton, carried a grudge for many years. In 1804 Burr challenged Hamilton to a duel, in which Hamilton was shot and killed.

The next contested election, in 1824, did not lead to bloodshed, although emotions ran equally high. The electoral college selected John Quincy Adams, whose father had been the second president, over Andrew Jackson. Jackson, a famous general, had won the popular vote and also was ahead after the first vote in the electoral college. But Henry Clay, who was not only a candidate but also the Speaker of the House, made a deal with Adams. Clay urged the representatives to support Adams. In return, President Adams named Clay as his secretary of state. Jackson got his revenge when he defeated Adams for the presidency in 1828.

Things were quiet for the electoral college for more than fifty years. Not until 1876, a decade after the Civil War, did another presidential election crisis erupt. Democratic governor Samuel J. Tilden of New York won the popular vote over Republican Rutherford B. Hayes of Ohio. Tilden seemed to be on his way to victory when several Southern states, still upset over their defeat in the Civil War, conspired to snatch victory away from him. Democratic ballots were thrown out in Louisiana, South Carolina, and Florida because of supposed fraud, violence, and intimidation against black voters. Republican officials "threw out" the votes in counties with especially bad records of violence and fraud. When these votes were thrown out, Hayes carried the three states. In a scene that was repeated 124 years later, both candidates sent lawyers to Florida to file lawsuits contesting the vote. After the disputes were settled, the electoral count ended up in a tie. Congress set up a commission of eight Republicans and seven Democrats to select the winner. The Republicans voted as a group, and Rutherford B. Hayes was selected as the seventeenth president of the United States—just three days before his inauguration.

In 1888 the most popular candidate again did not become president. Grover Cleveland, who was running for reelection, was able to get 91,000 more popular votes than his challenger, Indiana senator Benjamin Harrison. But Cleveland lost in the electoral college by a large margin, 233 to 168, and Harrison was declared the winner, despite widespread charges of fraud by Cleveland supporters. Although there were several close presidential elections in the years that followed, most notably in 1948 when Harry Truman beat Thomas Dewey and in 1960 when John Kennedy beat Richard Nixon, it was not until the new millennium when Bush beat Gore that history repeated itself.

The controversy began on election night when the national television networks reported that Gore had won the state of Florida and probably the presidency. A few hours later the same networks said they had made a mistake. They declared Bush the winner in Florida and the next president of the United States. Gore even called George W. at about two o'clock in the morning to congratulate him.

But the television networks were wrong again. The Florida vote was too close to call, and court orders

On November 8, 2000, U.S. voters were still waiting to learn the results of the previous day's election. They would wait for more than a month.

were obtained to count the ballots by hand. For more than a month, local, state, and federal judges were asked to decide who had actually won the election. It wasn't until December 12, 2000, that the U.S. Supreme Court's historic and controversial decision finally awarded the presidency to George W. Bush.

The election controversies hurt George W. politically because many people questioned the legitimacy of the election and the Supreme Court ruling. The focus on Bush's difficulties in getting elected also diminished the historic nature of his accomplishment. George W.'s election was only the second time the son of a former president was elected to the nation's highest office and only the fifth time in U.S. history that a president was elected despite losing the popular vote to his opponent. More important, the disputed election overshadowed the remarkable personal and professional changes that George W. had undergone to become president.

George W. views the world from the shoulders of his proud father. Family members nicknamed them "Big George" and "Little George."

Chapter **ONE**

BIG GEORGE, LITTLE GEORGE

WHEN GEORGE W. BUSH WAS RUNNING FOR president of the United States, he liked to present himself as a Texan, a "good ol' boy" who liked to eat chili and wear cowboy hats and cowboy boots. He was proud of the fact, he said, that he had nothing in common with the East Coast preppies (such as his opponent Al Gore) whose families ran the government and the financial centers of power in Washington, D.C., and New York City.

But George W. actually had much more in common with those folks than he let on. For example, although Bush was the governor of Texas and spoke with a Texas twang, he was not a native Texan. George W. was born thousands of miles away from the Lone Star

A young George W., shown with his parents and paternal grandparents, right, *already wears the cowboy boots of a Texan.*

State. Little George, as he was known in childhood, was born on July 6, 1946, on the East Coast in New Haven, Connecticut. Like Gore, whose father was a United States senator from Tennessee, George W. was born into a powerful political family. His grandfather was Prescott Bush, a United States senator from Connecticut. Other relatives were bankers and Wall Street stockbrokers. The Bush family could trace their ancestry back to the fourteenth century, "making him a fourteenth cousin to Queen Elizabeth II and a relative of the entire British royal family."

In the Bush family, Big George was George Herbert Walker Bush, George W.'s father. When Little George was born, his father was finishing his education at Yale University after serving in World War II. Big George met Barbara Pierce, a distant relative of former president Franklin Pierce, at a country club dance in Greenwich, Connecticut, in 1941. The couple became engaged two years later, in 1943, while Big George was a fighter pilot in the United States Navy. In 1944, while on a bombing mission, his plane was shot down. He parachuted out of the plane, landing in shark-infested waters before being rescued. A few months later he returned home to a hero's welcome. Dressed in his navy uniform, Big George married Barbara on January 6, 1945. On his forehead was a large bandage, hiding a cut he'd received while jumping from his burning airplane.

After graduation from Yale University in 1948, Big George faced a tough choice. He could follow his father and family into the world of business and politics on the East Coast, or he could set off in a completely new direction. Big George decided to set off on his own. He moved his young family to western Texas, where one of the greatest oil booms in

Barbara and George Herbert Walker Bush on their wedding day in 1945

history was starting. Seeking to cash in on the boom, Big George took a job as a clerk with one of the oil drilling companies in the area. He rented a small apartment in a tough neighborhood in the city of Odessa. It was all Big George could afford on a monthly salary of $375.

A year later the company moved the family to California, where George W.'s sister Pauline Robinson (whom everyone called Robin) was born in 1949. The family returned to Texas the next year, settling in Midland, a dusty little town full of tumbleweeds and rattlesnakes, seemingly in the middle of nowhere. Midland, however, was the center of the oil boom. So big was the boom that the town soon became the richest in the country. It boasted more Rolls Royce luxury cars per person than anywhere else in the United States. A few years after arriving, Big George started his own oil company, the Zapata Petroleum Corporation, named after the famous Mexican revolutionary Emiliano Zapata. Bush decided on the name after seeing a popular movie called *Viva Zapata,* starring Marlon Brando.

The success of Zapata Petroleum allowed the Bush family to buy their first house, a two-bedroom home on a street nicknamed "Easter Egg Row." The houses were built so much alike that the owners painted them bright colors to tell them apart. The Bush home was painted bright blue and cost $7,500. Within a couple of years, as Zapata Petroleum became more

A long way from his East Coast upbringing, Big George, right, *seeks his fortune in the Texas oil fields. In 1956 little George,* left, *attended the opening ceremony for a new offshore drilling platform with his dad.*

successful, the family moved to a better neighborhood and a better house, this one with a swimming pool.

Friends and relatives remember George W. as being an extremely active child. He was the class clown, always cracking jokes and wanting to be the center of attention—traits he carried with him throughout his life. Living in Midland suited young George W. He attended Sam Houston Elementary School. He passed his days swimming in the pool, riding bikes, climbing behind the bleachers at Friday night football games, playing catcher on his Little League baseball team, and attending family barbecues. Bush recalls that neighbors watched out for each other. He remembers when a friend's mother caught him crossing the street without looking both ways. The mom yelled at him as if he were her own son, then lectured him not to do it again.

"Midland was a small town with small-town values," George W. recalled. "We learned to respect our elders, to do what they said, and to be good neighbors. We went to church. Families spent time together, outside, the grown-ups talking with neighbors while the kids played ball or with marbles and yo-yos. No one locked their doors, because you could trust your friends and neighbors. It was a happy childhood. I was surrounded by love and friends and sports."

But life in Midland was not without tragedy for George W. In October 1953, his sister Robin died of cancer. Robin had begun feeling ill in February, about the same time the Bush's third child, John (Jeb), was born. The family would eventually include Neil (born in 1955), Marvin (born in 1956), and Dorothy (born in 1959). During the time Robin was sick, Big George and Barbara decided not to tell their eldest son how seriously ill his sister had become. It was a tough choice, but as Barbara Bush said years later, "We thought he was too young to cope."

Little George discovered how serious the illness had been while at school one day. His parents, who had been in New York with Robin while she received treatment, drove to pick him up two days after the three-year-old girl had died in New York. George W., who was in the second grade, was taking a record player to the principal's office with a friend when he saw his parents' car. He ran to a teacher to tell her that he had to go because his parents and sister were waiting for him. "I run over to the car and there's no Robin," Bush recalled.

It was then that his parents told him what had happened. "I was sad, and stunned," Bush later said. "I knew Robin had been sick, but death was hard for me to imagine. Minutes before, I had had a little sister, and now, suddenly, I did not. Forty-six years later, those minutes remain my starkest memory of my childhood, a sharp pain in the midst of an otherwise happy blur."

Little George W. poses with his younger sister Robin and their father.

The boy was very upset, not only by the death but because his parents had not told him how sick Robin had been. For a long time George W., who was seven when Robin died, had nightmares about his sister's death.

Little George's parents also wondered if they'd done the right thing by not telling him how ill Robin had been. They said they did not want to burden him with such terrible news because there was nothing he could do.

Barbara Bush said later, "I don't know if that was right or wrong, but he said to me several times, 'You know, why didn't you tell me?'"

George W.'s parents also felt Robin's loss. Barbara Bush went into a depression. Her hair turned white before she was thirty years old from the strain of coping with the loss. People visiting the house, even George W.'s young friends, noticed how sad George W.'s mom had become. Eventually people did not mention Robin's name inside the Bush home.

George W. finally broke the sadness in the household and brought some needed laughter to his parents without intending to. George had just learned about how the Earth spins on its axis, when one day after school, he asked his mother which way Robin had been buried in her grave.

"What difference would it make?" his mother asked him.

"One way she'd be spinning like this," he said, demonstrating by turning himself around in one di-

George W. smiles with his parents in Rye, New York, during the summer of 1955. George W. had the ability to lighten the mood, even as the family dealt with the tragic loss of Robin.

rection, "and one way like this," he said, reversing direction.

Another time George W. attended a football game with his father and some of his friends. When the boy's vision was blocked by adults, he turned to his father and said he wished he were dead like his sister Robin up in heaven. After a brief silence, the father asked his son why. "I bet," Little George said smiling, "she can see the game better from up there than we can here."

George W.'s 1964 yearbook photo at Phillips Academy in Andover, Massachusetts, his senior year

Chapter **TWO**

SCHOOL DAZE

THE SMALL-TOWN LIFESTYLE THAT GEORGE W. ENJOYED in Midland changed dramatically in 1959. After serving as class president and quarterback of the football team, he and his family moved to Houston, one of the biggest cities in the country. George W.'s father wanted to get into politics, and he thought business and political prospects were brighter in the big city. Little George quickly made friends. He became a class officer at the private Kincaid School and also joined the school football team. The friendships he made while in Houston were so strong that many friends stayed with him in important jobs all the way to the White House.

The most important event in George W.'s young life took place in 1961, when his parents sent him away from home for the first time. George Herbert Walker Bush had graduated from Phillips Academy in Andover, Massachusetts, and he and Barbara wanted their son to follow in his footsteps. They took him on a visit to Andover and enrolled him in the private academy. The move marked a turning point in George W.'s life because he had to make his way without his family for the first time. He and his friends didn't understand why he had to go away to Andover.

"'Bush, what did you do wrong?' a friend in Houston had asked, only somewhat jokingly, upon hearing I was going away to boarding school," Bush recalled. "In those days, Texas boys who got shipped off to boarding school were usually in trouble with their parents. In my case, Andover was a family tradition; my parents wanted me to learn not only the academics but also how to thrive on my own."

The fact that George W. was doing something for his parents and something they believed to be for his own good did not make his time at Andover any easier. "Forlorn is the best way to describe my sense of the place and my initial attitude," Bush said about arriving at Andover. "Andover was cold and distant and difficult. In every way it was a long way from home."

George W.'s stay was made more difficult because his dad was something of a legend at the school. His father had been a star athlete, a near perfect student, and president of the senior class. Upon graduating, the elder Bush had delayed going to college so he could enlist in the military, becoming the youngest pilot in the United States Navy in World War II. When he returned home, he attended Yale University, and after graduation he started his own company. This was the legacy fifteen-year-old George W. had to live up to when he entered Phillips Academy.

"Throughout his days, George W. would be trailed by the halo and shadow of his father," writes biographer Elizabeth Mitchell, who covered the Bush family for many years. "Some of the twinning of mannerisms could be downright spooky to friends...[and] of course, they shared the same first and last names. People were always doing somersaults to distinguish between the two of them." The comparisons started almost as soon as George W. arrived at Phillips.

What people at Phillips most remember about George W. was his love of stickball. Stickball, similar to baseball, is a game played in streets or small areas. A broom handle or other long wooden stick is used to bat a small rubber ball to score runs. George W. created a stickball league and got everyone on campus to join. He named himself commissioner of the league and set up a schedule of games and play-offs. George W., who was sometimes mistakenly called Junior, also played varsity basketball and baseball. He was not considered a star on the field, but he worked hard.

George W. did not do well in the classroom. In fact, he did so badly that he was afraid he was going to flunk out of school. The first essay he wrote in an

George W., front row center, **played on the Phillips Academy baseball team.**

English class was a complete failure. George W. misused big words he did not understand, and the teacher gave him a zero on his report. "And my math grades weren't all that good either," Bush said years later. "So I was struggling."

Although Bush never made the honor roll, he was popular on campus. He made friends easily and earned the nickname "Lip" because he had an opinion on just about everything and often spoke sharply. He became the head cheerleader for the football team at the all-boys school. He also was a member of a rock-and-roll band called the Torqueys. George W. didn't play an instrument. His job was to stand on stage and clap his hands. When he graduated from Phillips, he was popular enough to finish second in the election for Big Man on Campus.

"George and I are both witness to the fact that Andover has such an excellent academic system, and even people at bottom tier—where I was and George was—can be okay and go to good colleges," said classmate Don Vermeil.

After graduation from Phillips Academy, Bush had to decide which college to attend. Although he did not seem to enjoy being away from home or being on the East Coast, he wanted to follow in his father's footsteps and go to Yale. It did not appear that George W. had the grades to get into such a prestigious school, however. George W. applied there anyway, but he also applied to the University of Texas, a good school but with less strict entrance requirements than Yale.

As critics would point out later, his family's connections rescued George W. Both his father and his grandfather had gone to Yale. Because he was the relative of Yale graduates, George W. was admitted to the university to keep the family tradition, or legacy, alive.

George W. set off for Yale in the fall of 1964 to study history. He soon found himself in the middle of history.

On and off the field, George W. was an enthusiastic participant in Phillips athletics. He is shown here cheering the football team.

As a student at Yale University, George W. was often annoyed by the school's elite Ivy League atmosphere, despite his own distinguished family history.

Chapter THREE

THE LAST OF THE SHORT HAIRS

GEORGE W. ARRIVED AT YALE IN **1964** DURING the Vietnam War and at the beginning of a cultural upheaval. The radicalism, the antiwar protests, the drug use, and the alternative lifestyles that came to symbolize the 1960s were in their early stages. By the time Bush and his classmates graduated in the spring of 1968, the country had experienced dramatic changes.

"We later joked that members of the class of 1968 were the last in a long time to have short hair," Bush said. Despite his ability to laugh about his time at Yale, George W. was not happy with the school. He believed Yale and many other Ivy League schools harbored what he called intellectual snobs, people who thought they were smarter than everybody else. George W. also thought the university had never given his father the respect he deserved. "I was irritated at Yale," Bush said. "I just can't believe the university would not be bending over backwards to say to one of the most distinguished alumnus they've had, that they're going to . . . give this man an honor and treat him with utmost respect. Maybe that's not fair to the institution for me to feel that way, but I feel that way."

George W.'s anger began soon after arriving on campus, when he met one of the leading Yale intellectuals, the Reverend William Sloane Coffin, who had attended the school with George W.'s father. Coffin was the chaplain at Yale and a protester against the Vietnam War.

George W. introduced himself to his father's old classmate just after the elder Bush had been defeated in the Texas senate race by Senator Ralph Yarborough, a liberal Democrat. George W. said he remembers Coffin telling him, "I know your father and your father lost to a better man."

Coffin insists that he does not remember the incident. And if it did happen, he said, he was probably kidding. "I knew he wasn't kidding," George W. said. "He might have been kidding—I just didn't pick up on his sense of humor."

George W. was deeply offended by what Coffin had said, believing the comment was a personal attack against his father. The comment not only awakened a deep desire in George W. to protect his father, but it

George W. felt that the Reverend William Sloane Coffin, left, *insulted his father during a brief run-in on Yale University's campus. An active antiwar protester, Coffin was later tried on charges of conspiring to aid young men in dodging the draft.*

also fueled George W.'s growing dislike of Ivy League intellectuals.

"I've been turned off by intellectual snobbery most of my life," George W. has said. "Once you go to those schools and can compete academically, you realize that these people . . . really are quite shallow. Just because you've got a big university by your name doesn't mean you're any smarter or any brighter than somebody else, necessarily. It matters how you apply your education. I don't remember spending a lot of my time brooding or walking around with a dark cloud over my head thinking, 'Oh there's another unbelievably shallow intellectual.' But there's pretentiousness. I think one of the things that people have found out about me, and maybe a lot has to do with how I was raised and who raised me, is that I am an unpretentious person."

Unassuming and unpretentious are good words to describe George W. at Yale. He wore rumpled clothes and drove an old, beat-up car. He seems to have made as little impact at Yale as he did at Andover. Most of his teachers don't remember him being involved in campus social and academic activities. Instead, Bush focused his time on intramural sports and partying. As a freshman, he was a pitcher on the Yale baseball team, and he took up rugby two years later.

While at Yale, Bush developed a drinking problem. Bush joined the Delta Kappa Epsilon (DKE) fraternity, known as the biggest-drinking, loudest-partying house on campus, geared mainly toward athletes. The fraternity brothers at DKE did some outrageous stunts and got into occasional problems with authorities. Bush, who became president of the fraternity just as his father had, was often in the middle of the pranks. One night while walking home from a party where he had drunk too much, he suddenly lay down in the middle of the street and rolled himself home. While attending a football game at Princeton, Bush and some friends tore down the goalpost after Yale beat Princeton to win the Ivy League championship. "We charged onto the field to take the goal post down," Bush recalled. "Unfortunately, I was sitting on the crossbar when campus security arrived. The police were not nearly as impressed with our victory as we were. We were escorted off the field and told to leave town. I have not been back since."

That wasn't Bush's only brush with the law in college. During the Christmas holidays one year, in what Bush describes as "the infamous Christmas wreath caper," police arrested Bush and some friends for stealing a wreath from a department store. Bush claims the group was "liberating" or borrowing the wreath. He was charged with disorderly conduct, but the charge was eventually dropped after Bush and the others apologized for what they had done.

Friends say that while Bush had a wild side as a young man, he never did anything bad enough to prevent him from one day becoming president of the United States. In fact, they say, most of the things that Bush got involved with can probably be blamed on a combination of too much alcohol and not enough maturity.

"George was a fraternity guy," said Calvin Hill, a DKE brother who went on to play professional football with the Dallas Cowboys. "He [Bush] went through that stage in his life with a lot of joy, but I don't remember George as a chronic drunk. He was a good-time guy. But he wasn't the guy hugging the commode at the end of the day."

Friends recall Bush as being popular but going on only a few dates. He did get into some serious trouble with his father because of a girl, however. One summer while in college, George W. got a job on an oil rig in the Gulf of Mexico. He was dating a girl in Houston at the time and missed being with her. Since he would be heading back to college soon, he wanted to spend more time with her. So he quit his job and returned to Houston to be with her. His father was not amused. He called George W. into his Houston office and told his son how disappointed he was with the choice the young man had made.

George W. broke up with that girl a short time later but eventually found a new romance. During the Christmas break of his junior year at Yale, Bush got engaged to Cathryn Wolfman, a student at Rice University in Houston. Bush was twenty, the same age his father had been when he'd become engaged. However, George W.'s engagement to Wolfman ended quietly the following year as the couple drifted apart.

While college students across the country were marching for civil rights and against the Vietnam War, the most serious controversy Bush engaged in during his time at Yale was the fraternity's practice of "branding" pledges who wanted to join DKE. Bush and his fraternity brothers used a piece of heated metal to burn, or brand, the skin of prospective members. When the practice became public in 1967, it created a national story. In a much-publicized article in the *New York Times*, Bush defended the practice by saying the branding wounds were no worse than cigarette burns.

Although George W. was far different from his father at Yale, he did follow the elder Bush in one respect:

Like his father and grandfather, George W. was a member of Yale's Skull and Bones Society. Note the lack of windows in the secret society's meetinghouse.

joining the secret Skull and Bones Society on campus. His father had been a famous baseball player and war hero when selected to join the elite group. Each year the group chose and accepted the top fifteen Yale students. Although George W. was not among them, he was allowed to join Skull and Bones as a "legacy," a recruit whose father had been a Bonesman. He was allowed his membership to maintain the family tradition. Bonesmen are sworn to secrecy about what takes place during their meetings, but some members have talked anonymously to journalists over the years. While many members agonized over what they would do when drafted, what they remember about Bush is how passionately he defended his father, who supported the Vietnam War.

While George W. spent his time partying at Yale without a care in the world, the world began to nudge him and his fraternity brothers during their senior year. In 1968 the Reverend Martin Luther King Jr. was assassinated, as was Senator Robert Kennedy a few months later. The killings left many college students angry. At the same time, more and more U.S. soldiers were dying in Vietnam as the war escalated in Southeast Asia.

"The events of 1968 rocked our previously placid world and shocked the country, Yale, and me," Bush recalled. "In many ways that spring was the end of an era of innocence. The gravity of history was beginning to descend in a horrifying and disruptive way." By the time George W. graduated with a degree in history, he and his friends had to confront the Vietnam War head-on. Upon graduation they were required to register for the draft and risk being sent to fight in Vietnam. "The war was no longer something that was happening to other people in a distant land; it came home to us," Bush said. "We didn't have the luxury of looking for a job or taking time to consider what to do next. We were more concerned with the decision that each of us had to make: military service or not."

Thousands of young men faced with such a tough decision decided to leave the United States and head to Canada to avoid the draft. Bush, whose father was by then a congressman, said he never considered such a choice. "I knew I would serve," Bush said. "Leaving the country to avoid the draft was not an option for me; I was too conservative and too traditional. My inclination was to support the government and the war until proven wrong, and that only came later."

Bush, however, found a way to serve without being sent to Vietnam. He joined the Texas Air National Guard. Bush applied in Houston and was accepted almost immediately. The enlistment proved a very controversial decision for both the National Guard and the future presidential candidate.

Although his service in the Texas Air National Guard was viewed by critics as a way to escape combat in Vietnam, George W. says that he just wanted to be a military pilot.

Chapter **FOUR**

THE WILD BLUE YONDER

THE ENLISTMENT OF GEORGE W. BUSH IN THE Air National Guard was bound to draw attention, and it did. In joining the guard, George W. followed the sons of many prominent families in Texas. These young men had found a way to perform their military service without risking their lives in combat. The guard was a reserve group stationed in the United States. The guard also flew older jets, which meant that even if the unit was called to Vietnam, it probably would not fight.

Charges were soon raised that because Bush was a congressman's son, he had gotten preferential treatment, leapfrogging ahead of more deserving candidates. Congressman Bush's district included the

Houston area, where George W. had signed up. Also, George W. had scored the lowest acceptable grade on the pilot aptitude test, much lower than other more qualified—but rejected—candidates had done on the entrance exam. Later, a concern was raised about the fact that Bush had not filled out the section on the application asking about past illegal activity. "While the pilot training and Air National Guard service that followed were by no means easy, pleasant experiences, they were a far cry from being sent into the infantry. . . . That meant that George W. got exactly the military situation he was looking for, an uncommon luxury in that era," wrote Elizabeth Mitchell, a Bush biographer.

George W.'s response to all the criticism was that he had probably just forgotten to fill in the illegal activity section of the application. He denied that Texas politicians and friends of his father "pulled strings" to get him accepted. The enlistment required two years of training and four years of part-time duty. Bush said most men didn't want to be in the military that long, so there were fighter-pilot openings in the guard. He insisted that he would have gone to Vietnam if ordered to do so. Bush said he chose the guard not to avoid combat but because it was the quickest way to become a military pilot like his father.

"I was well aware of my dad's service as a navy fighter pilot in World War II. . . . " Bush said. "I'm sure the fact that my dad had been a fighter pilot influenced

The elder Bush proudly presents his son with the bars signifying his promotion to second lieutenant in the Air National Guard. The occasion was highly publicized by George W.'s unit commander.

my thinking. I remember him telling me how much he loved to fly, how exhilarating the experience of piloting a plane was. I was headed for the military, and I wanted to learn a new skill that would make doing my duty an interesting adventure. I had never flown an airplane but decided I wanted to become a pilot."

Regardless of how Bush got into the guard, the unit commander, Colonel Walter B. "Buck" Staudt, made sure everyone in Houston knew about it. Bush was sworn in on the same day he applied, but Colonel Staudt held a special ceremony weeks later so journalists could photograph him with the congressman's son. When George W. was later promoted to lieutenant, Staudt held another ceremony for the newspapers.

This time Staudt invited Congressman Bush, who flew from Washington to Houston to be photographed with his son and the colonel.

The notoriety continued. As the political career of George W.'s father advanced, people also took notice of his eldest son. Congressman Bush had campaigned for Richard Nixon in Texas during the 1968 presidential race. When elected, Nixon had rewarded Bush by appointing him to several important political posts, including U.S. ambassador to the United Nations in 1970 and chairman of the Republican National Committee in 1973. Critics say that because of this relationship, George W. was allowed to do things other servicemen could not. A few months after enlisting,

Tricia Nixon, one of President Richard Nixon's daughters, in 1969. President Nixon flew George W. to Washington for a date with his daughter.

for example, George W. was allowed to take a two-month leave to work for a Republican candidate in Florida. The next year, while George W. was still in training, President Nixon sent a special air force plane to Georgia, where Bush was stationed, to fly the young man to Washington for a date with the president's daughter Tricia.

George W. in a casual moment with his father and brothers in 1970. Left to right: *Neil, George, Jeb, and George W.*

Chapter **FIVE**

THE SCHOOL OF HARD KNOCKS

THE **HIGH-PROFILE DATE WITH THE PRESIDENT'S** daughter gave George W. a reputation as a ladies' man. Like other pilots, George W. was known as someone who liked to work hard and play hard, a lifestyle that only intensified as Bush went on weekend, or part-time, duty in 1970 after graduating from training school on June 23. Having so much free time was not a good thing for George W. His life got even wilder as he entered what he called his irresponsible, or no-madic, years, when his life drifted without direction.

Bush was one of the most eligible bachelors in Texas, and he seems to have enjoyed that reputation. The twenty-four-year-old Bush rented a one-bedroom apartment in a Houston complex that was popular

with singles. He played all-day games of pool volley-
ball with other residents in one of the complex's six
swimming pools.

In 1971 President Nixon named the elder Bush to be
the U.S. representative to the United Nations in New
York. The Bush family moved to New York, but
George W. stayed in Houston. A family friend, Robert
H. Dow, hired George W. to work at a company selling
agricultural products. It was the first nine-to-five,
coat-and-tie job George W. had ever held, and he
hated it. He stayed there only about nine months.

*In the early 1970s, as George W. tried to find out what path he
wanted to take in life, his father's political career was taking off.
Here the elder Bush,* right, *appears with Texas gubernatorial
candidate Paul Eggers,* left, *and Republican president Richard
Nixon,* center, *at a campaign rally.*

At this point, George W. toyed with the idea of running for the Texas legislature. His family name was well known in Houston, and the newspapers soon heard about his plan. The *Houston Post,* among others, wrote a story about the younger Bush wanting to get into politics, erroneously identifying George W. as George Bush Jr.

In the meantime, President Nixon asked the elder Bush to become chairman of the Republican National Committee, one of the most important political jobs in the country. In 1973 the Bush family moved to Washington, D.C. After spending the fall working on the campaign of Winton "Red" Blount, a conservative Republican running for the U.S. Senate in Alabama, George W. went to visit his family at Christmas. While there, he got into a drunken confrontation with his father that helped the young man find some direction.

The argument began after George W. took his sixteen-year-old brother, Marvin, out drinking. George W. was driving home when he ran over a neighbor's garbage can. The can stuck under the car, but George W. kept driving, producing a terrible racket. When he pulled up to his parents' house, the elder Bush awoke to find out what was going on. He naturally became upset when he saw what condition his sons, the car, and the garbage can were in. An argument followed between George W. and his father. At one point George W., after being brought inside the house, challenged his father to go outside and fight man-to-man.

The elder Bush was able to calm George W. down, but the incident troubled the father.

After quitting his agricultural sales job, George W. had decided to return to school to get his graduate degree. He wanted to become a lawyer and had applied to the University of Texas Law School, but his application was rejected. He then applied to Harvard Business School, one of the most prestigious schools in the country. But, if accepted, George W. would not start classes until September, more than nine months away. The elder Bush worried that his son might get into more trouble, so he arranged to have George W. do community work in one of Houston's poorest neighborhoods.

George W. was hired as a counselor in Professional United Leadership League (PULL), an inner-city youth program. PULL had been started by John L. White, a former professional football player, to provide mentors to inner-city minority kids. The program helped teenagers seventeen and under by providing them with counseling and recreational programs. The kids played sports, learned arts and crafts, and hung out in an old warehouse that the organization owned. George W. was a counselor in the program, and during the summer of 1973 Marvin Bush joined his older brother. They were the only white people working in the building. "They stood out like sore thumbs," said Muriel Simmons Henderson, another counselor. "John White was a good friend of their father. He told us that the father wanted George W. to see the other side of life. He asked John if he would put him in there."

George W. proved a huge success with the kids and his coworkers. He wrestled with the kids, played basketball with them, and took them on field trips. George W. found it easy to relate to the children because in many ways he was still a big, fun-loving kid himself. Coworkers remember Bush driving around in a beat-up old car. Bush had so many clothes and papers in the car that no one else could fit inside it. "He was a super, super guy," said Ernie Ladd, a former professional football player and professional wrestler. "If he was a stinker, I'd say he was a stinker. But everybody loved him so much. He had a way with people."

Ernie Ladd worked with George W. at Professional United Leadership League. He was impressed with George's way with people.

The experience also made quite an impression on George W. He recalls the sadness he felt at seeing how hard the lives of the kids were. On one occasion, a boy no more than eleven or twelve years old was playing basketball with George W. When the child jumped to shoot the ball, a loaded pistol fell out of his pocket. The child thought he needed the gun for protection.

George also found some happiness. He remembers befriending a boy named Jimmy, who became like a little brother to him. Each day the boy waited for George W. to arrive and then followed him everywhere. One day Jimmy showed up at the center without shoes, so George bought him a pair. He recalls that when he walked the boy home, Jimmy's mother was high on drugs.

"Jimmy was happy to be home, but I was incredibly sad to leave him there," Bush said. "My job gave me a glimpse of a world I had never seen. It was tragic, heartbreaking, and uplifting all at the same time. I saw a lot of poverty. I also saw bad choices: drugs, alcohol, abuse. . . . I saw children who could not read or write and were way behind in school. I also saw good and decent people working to try to help lift these kids out of their terrible circumstances," Bush said.

While at PULL, Bush received notice that he had been accepted to Harvard. He was enjoying his work with the kids so much that he thought about staying with the program, but John White convinced him to go to Harvard. "If you really care about these kids as much as I think you do, why don't you go and learn more and then you can really help," White told Bush.

Bush arrived at Harvard looking for some direction in his life. "I had learned to fly jets and acquired a good education," Bush recalled. "I had not yet settled on a path in my life." Harvard is a place where many of the future business leaders of the country were taught. But the twenty-seven-year-old Bush looked nothing like a slick Wall Street stockbroker or the son of a famous politician. Bush arrived at the school driving his dumpy car and sporting his usual casual clothes and attitude. In one famous yearbook photo George W. is shown sitting at the back of a classroom, dressed in a badly wrinkled shirt, casually chewing gum and blowing a large bubble.

Despite the casual attitude, George W. took his studies seriously. He learned about finance, marketing, and other things needed to run a business. He graduated with his master's degree in business administration and then surprised many people when he followed the path his father had taken more than twenty-five years earlier. George W. loaded up his car and drove west to the oil fields of Texas to make his fortune.

Workers tend to a Texas oil rig. Midland's oil production boomed in the 1970s.

Chapter **SIX**

OIL'S WELL
THAT ENDS
WELL?

ALTHOUGH HIS FATHER HAD BEEN IN THE OIL business, George W. had no experience running an oil company. He had his master's degree in business administration from Harvard, but George W. did the smart thing—he started at the bottom and worked his way up.

In 1975 George W. started out by working as a land man, looking up records in county courthouses around Texas to see who owned what properties. He then tried to get the owners to lease or sell the land to a company drilling for oil. George W.'s engaging personality served him well. He was able to drive up to homes and start conversations with complete strangers. Bush got enough experience to start his own oil company later.

At about the same time, Bush decided to run for Congress in 1977. He had worked on some of his father's races, so he had a good idea of what was involved in running a campaign. A popular Democratic congressman from the area had decided to retire unexpectedly. Bush, seeing an opportunity to win the seat for the Republican Party, decided to run in the Republican primary—an election to choose which candidates from a particular party will run in the general election. His father was delighted that his eldest son was following the family traditions and entering politics. George W.'s family and friends, including Joe O'Neill and Don Evans, were eager to help. Karl Rove, who had worked for George W.'s father, also went to Midland to help. Neil Bush, who had recently graduated from college, joined the campaign too.

In August, the same month George W. announced his congressional candidacy, Joe O'Neill and his wife, Jan, invited him to a barbecue. There, he met Laura Welch, a quiet elementary school librarian with no interest in politics. The unlikely couple was attracted to each other and went out the following night to play miniature golf. George took Laura to Houston, Texas, in October to meet his family. Less than three months later, on November 5, 1977, George and Laura were married at the First United Methodist Church in Midland. "If it wasn't love at first sight, it happened shortly thereafter," Bush said about meeting his wife.

George W. and Laura Bush on their wedding day, November 5, 1977. Left to right: **Marvin, Dorothy, Neil, Columb (Jeb's wife), Jeb, Laura, George W., Barbara, George, and Dorothy Walker Bush**

"My wife is gorgeous, good-humored, quick to laugh, down-to-earth, and very smart. I recognized those attributes right away in roughly that order."

Shortly after the wedding, George W. went back to his campaign but promised Laura that she would not have to make any speeches. A few months later, however, a terrified Laura made her first campaign speech in Muleshoe, Texas. In June 1978, George won the Republican primary election and began his campaign for the November general election.

The general election against Kent Hance, George W.'s Democratic opponent, proved to be educational. Despite Bush's prior experience, he was not prepared for the Hance campaign. Hance painted the younger Bush as an outsider to Texas, pointing out that the young man had been born in Connecticut and had gone to school back east at Phillips, Yale, and Harvard. Hance said that his own father and grandfather had been farmers in Texas for decades before the

Newlyweds George W. and Laura campaigned side by side when George W. ran for Congress. Despite their hard work, he lost the election.

Bush family showed up. Hance easily won the election.

After the lost election, Bush decided to get back into the oil business in Midland, where he'd grown up. He started his own oil-drilling company, which he called Arbusto—Spanish for "bush" or "shrub." He was aided in starting the company by family friends, who helped him to raise millions of dollars to buy equipment, lease offices, and hire workers. He proved to be a good boss, according to former workers. He treated people fairly and stayed out of the way of the technical people who actually decided where to drill for oil. Bush and his company enjoyed some success while the price of oil remained relatively high in the early 1980s.

In 1980 George took a break from business to devote himself to his father's primary campaign for the Republican nomination for president. The elder Bush had decided to enter the Republican primary in an effort to defeat incumbent president Jimmy Carter in the general election. Carter, a peanut farmer and former governor from Georgia, had become unpopular partly because of the economic problems the country was experiencing—problems such as oil shortages, high gasoline prices, inflation, and high unemployment. Adding to the problem, 444 U.S. citizens had been taken hostage by Iranian terrorists on November 4, 1979, and they were still being held at the U.S. embassy in Iran. The hostages had been held for more than a year, while unsuccessful attempts to free them weakened Carter politically and made him vulnerable in the 1980 presidential election.

Jeb Bush, left, enthusiastically applauds as his father delivers a speech during the 1980 presidential primary campaign. Neil Bush and his fiancée, Sharon Hart, look on during the event.

Although the elder Bush did not win the Republican nomination for president, the eventual nominee, Ronald Reagan, did select him as his vice presidential running mate. In the November general election, the Reagan-Bush ticket won the presidency.

George W. and Laura attended the presidential inauguration in January 1981. When his father took the oath of office as vice president of the United States, George W. was filled with pride. He felt that same emotion the following November, when Laura gave birth to twin daughters. The happy parents named the girls Jenna Welch, for Laura's mother, and Barbara Pierce, for George W.'s mother. George W. helped with

George Bush is sworn in as vice president of the United States on January 20, 1981, as Barbara looks on.

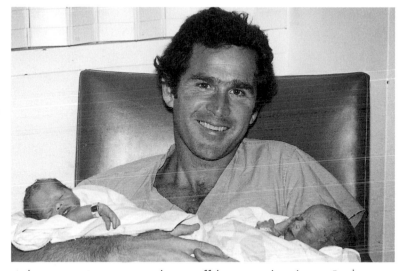

A beaming George W. shows off his twin daughters, Barbara Pierce, left, and Jenna Welch, right, born in November 1981.

the feeding and changing, and he took them for walks in the stroller.

In the meantime, George W. began thinking about getting back into a political race. He considered running for governor of Texas, which surprised his family. They wondered if he had the necessary experience for such a high office. Barbara Bush even told her son that he was probably not ready to run for that office. George W. was angry, but he wisely listened.

Instead of going into politics, George W. devoted himself to keeping his oil company in business. George was not as successful as his father had been, and by 1982 the oil industry began to go into a slump. In

1984 Bush merged Arbusto with a larger oil explo-
ration company called Spectrum 7. By 1985 the price
of oil had gone from $25 to $9 per barrel. Companies
and fortunes were wiped out. George W.'s company
was among those suffering in Texas. The company was
on the verge of bankruptcy, $1.6 million in debt in
1985. Luckily, Bush was once again rescued by his
name and family connections. "I'm all name and no
money," George W. was heard to say while looking for
someone to bail out his company.

The rescuer was a big company named Harken Oil
and Gas. The company wanted to use the Bush name
and George W.'s family connections. So Harken
bought Spectrum 7 in 1986 and paid off the company's $3.1 million in debt. Harken also hired many
of the former Spectrum employees. Bush was hired as
a consultant for $120,000 a year while he was working
full time on his father's presidential campaign. He
also received $300,000 of Harken stock and was made
a member of its board of directors.

"What was Harken getting for its money? The son of
the vice president of the United States," the founder
of Harken answered when asked how the deal helped
Harken. "His name was George Bush. That was worth
the money they paid him."

When the Harken deal closed, Bush was able to walk
away with hundreds of thousands of dollars and the
possibility of making much more than that through a
stock plan. Although George W. was finally set finan-

cially, he once again had fallen short. Just as he had tried and failed to follow in his father's footsteps at Phillips Academy and Yale, George W. again failed to reach the kind of success his father had enjoyed in the oil business. But George W. did gain something besides money from his failure in the oil business. The business deal helped set him up for his next big venture: the world of professional baseball.

George Bush's workout routine is interrupted by a playful George W., wearing a Texas Rangers jacket.

Chapter **SEVEN**

HIGHBALLS AND HARDBALLS

BEFORE **GEORGE W. MOVED UP TO THE MAJOR** leagues, he had to deal with a major problem—his excessive drinking. The drinking had been bothering him and his family most of his adult life. On one occasion, George W. berated the *Wall Street Journal* writer Al Hunt, swearing at him in public. He frequently arrived at work hungover from the previous night's binge. Although Bush insists he was not an alcoholic, he also readily admits that he had a bad habit of drinking too much and then getting into arguments. That all changed when, at age forty, Bush decided that enough was enough. He vowed to give up drinking.

Laura had been trying to get her husband to quit drinking for years. When drinking, George W. often lost his temper, got into arguments, and said things that weren't as funny as he thought. A conversation with the Reverend Billy Graham, a family friend, got Bush thinking about making this life-altering decision. But it wasn't until the celebration of his fortieth birthday that Bush finally decided to quit drinking. George W., Laura, and some friends gathered at the Broadmoor Hotel in Colorado in June 1986 to celebrate several birthdays. The next morning Bush, an avid runner, went out for his usual jog. He felt so terrible that as he came back to shower, he decided his body was trying to tell him he was getting too old to drink. He decided to stop and claims he hasn't had a drink since.

The love and support of George W.'s family (shown here at George and Barbara Bush's home in Kennebunkport, Maine) helped him give up alcohol. George W. and Laura, with the twins, are the third and fourth adults from the left.

"There are turning points in life, and one of mine was quitting drinking, which I finally did shortly after my fortieth birthday. My wife and friends later joked that . . . I quit after seeing the bar bill," said Bush, who says it was not difficult to stop. "People later asked if something special happened, some incident, some argument or accident that turned the tide, but no. I just drank too much and woke up with a hangover."

After deciding to refrain from alcohol, Bush was faced with another tough decision. No longer working on a daily basis, he was once again looking for something to do with his life. In 1986 he joined his father's presidential campaign as an adviser. The elder Bush, after eight years of being vice president, was finally getting his chance to run for president in 1988. George W. served as his father's "enforcer" on the campaign trail. He insisted on complete loyalty to his father from the entire campaign staff. In trying to keep things running smoothly, George W. often got into yelling matches with workers and journalists which fueled his growing reputation of having a bad temper. He did so because he was obsessed with making sure campaign workers were loyal to his father and journalists were fair when writing about him.

He became especially angry when witty Ann Richards of Texas, the keynote speaker at the Democratic National Convention, portrayed the elder Bush as a weak politician who succeeded only because he had had things handed to him his whole life. She also

Ann Richards, then state treasurer of Texas, was the keynote speaker at the 1988 Democratic National Convention. She angered George W. with her public jokes about his father.

poked fun at his habit of mispronouncing words. During her speech on national television, Richards said it really wasn't his fault. "Poor George," she said, "he can't help it. He was born with a silver foot in his mouth." The memorable remark drew a huge laugh from the audience, but it also upset the Bush family, especially George W.

Despite his temper, people acknowledged that George W. was a hard worker who played an important role in getting his father elected president of the United States. His father's election victory made George W. better known around the country. Once again George W. toyed with the idea of getting into politics, possibly running for governor of Texas. He and his advisers decided a 1990 race would be too close to his father's election. Although George W. and his family occasionally visited the White House, W. consciously distanced himself from his father by not getting involved politically or getting appointed to any agency in his father's government. Most of his life, George W. had been fighting the perception that he had gotten where he was because of his father. If W. was to have any political future, he needed to do something to establish himself, so he decided to jump into the world of professional baseball. With a group of other men, he became part owner of the Texas Rangers.

George W. had always been a huge fan of major-league baseball. As a child, he had collected baseball cards, memorized statistics, and pretended to be Willie Mays, his favorite player. George W. recalled that the other kids in Midland were always impressed with his father's catching abilities. They especially liked the fact that Mr. Bush could catch a fly ball with his glove behind his back.

The group purchased the team for $75 million in 1989. Bush's part of the purchase price was $600,000. Bush was given a 10 percent stake in the team. Once

George W. took on a new project as part owner of the Texas Rangers baseball team.

again his primary benefit to the other investors was his name and family history.

George W. obtained the money for his part of the Rangers purchase by taking out a bank loan, using his Harken stock to guarantee the loan. In 1990 Bush sold 212,140 shares of that stock to pay off the loan. But the stock sale proved controversial. He sold the stock on June 22, 1990, when the company's stock price was $4 a share. Bush made $835,000 on the sale. Within two weeks, the stock price dropped to less then $2.50 a share.

The obvious question was whether Bush, who was on Harken's board of directors, had known about the financial problems before they became known to the public. Also, had he sold his stock based on that information to avoid the drop in stock price that would surely follow? This type of selling, called insider trading, is illegal. A complaint was lodged against Bush, and the Securities and Exchange Commission (SEC) investigated. The SEC is a federal agency that enforces the laws governing the purchase and sale of stocks and bonds.

George W. said he had not known about the company's financial difficulties. He insisted that he would not have sold the stock if he had known about the problems. He pointed out that Harken's lawyers had studied the sale and said it was okay. Bush also maintained that he hadn't found out about the financial problems until a month after he sold the stock. The government finally ended its investigation in 1993, deciding there was not enough evidence to charge Bush with any crime.

With his money secured, Bush went to work with the Texas Rangers, a team that had never had much success. The team played near Dallas, and their biggest star was the legendary pitcher Nolan Ryan. Bush's political advisers thought the purchase was a good move because it made Bush a famous Texas businessman. If Bush was serious about entering the 1994 Texas governor's race, being with the club would keep his name in the news on an almost daily basis.

Bush was asked to serve as the team's public spokesman and managing partner. The most significant thing the group did was to get a new $190 million stadium built in 1994. This greatly increased the value of the team and helped Bush prove that he could come through on a major project.

The job with the Rangers also helped the people of Texas to get to know George W. He had his mother, then the First Lady, throw out the first pitch at a

First Lady Barbara Bush throws the first pitch at a Rangers game in 1989.

George W. enjoys a day of fishing with his dad in Kennebunkport, Maine, in August 1991.

Rangers game. He spoke to community groups about the team every week and was in the stands for each home game. He signed thousands of autographs for fans and even got his boyhood dream fulfilled when the team issued a baseball card with his picture on it. While he was with the Rangers, Bush suffered only two big setbacks: the Rangers never won the World Series, and he was unsuccessful in getting his father reelected president. Bill Clinton defeated the elder Bush in 1992 by 43 percent to 38 percent of the vote.

On the campaign trail again, George W. runs for governor of Texas in 1994. Here he speaks to a crowd during a lunchtime campaign stop in Irving, Texas.

Chapter EIGHT

"W" STANDS FOR WINNER

IF IT WASN'T FOR ANN RICHARDS, THE HILARIOUS AND sharp-tongued former governor of Texas, there is a good chance that George W. Bush never would have become president of the United States. Some of George W.'s friends believe that one of the reasons he ran against Richards in 1994 was to get back at her for making fun of his father during the 1988 Democratic National Convention.

Despite being well known around the country and in Texas because of his identification with the Rangers, George W. realized he would have to be careful in his race against Richards. She was a popular governor, the most popular in thirty years. Richards also had a great sense of humor, which she displayed on television with

George W. faced a savvy, popular opponent in Ann Richards. The two went head-to-head during a gubernatorial debate on October 21, 1994.

talk-show hosts such as Jay Leno and David Letterman. Bush advisers feared that with her quick wit, Richards would make George W. so angry that he would embarrass himself. Bush and his people also knew that the biggest problem George W. faced was being seen as just another George Bush.

"My biggest problem in Texas is the question, 'What's the boy ever done? He could be riding his Daddy's name,'" Bush said prior to the campaign. George W. decided to address the issue directly. He told his parents to stay away from the press conference at which he announced his candidacy so they would not be the focus of attention. At his first campaign stop, he stated his reason for running for governor. "I am not running for governor because I am George Bush's son," he said. "I am running because I am Jenna and Barbara's father." Although George W. didn't let his father get involved in his campaign, his mother campaigned for him and for his brother Jeb, who was running for governor of Florida.

George W. Bush ran on the issues of decentralizing public education, toughening the juvenile justice system, and reforming the welfare system. He also played it smart throughout the campaign. As much as he disliked Ann Richards, Bush decided that the best way to defeat her was to be nice to her. "We're never going to attack her because she would be a fabulous victim," Bush told his advisers. "We're going to treat her with respect and dignity. This is how we are going to win." Bush didn't even show anger when Richards said George W. had gotten everything in life because of his father. Bush only criticized Richards's policies but let his campaign people criticize Richards.

The formula proved successful. Bush surprised many people around the country and won the election with 53 percent of the vote. Richards managed to get only 46 percent. Suddenly George W. Bush was the governor of one of the biggest states in the country, and he was seen in a new light. George W. quickly became a major national political force. All he had to do to remain a Republican power broker was to avoid doing anything foolish in office so people would continue to take him seriously. His brother Jeb, however, was not so lucky. Jeb lost the governor's race in Florida that year.

The entire Bush family gathered in Texas to see George W. get sworn in as governor. George W. was the first Republican to be elected governor of the state of Texas since 1877. George, Laura, and the twins moved to Austin, Texas, to live in the stately governor's mansion.

George W. proved to be an effective, but not spectacular, governor. He focused on harsher penalties for criminals, local control of education, cutting welfare, protecting corporations from big lawsuits, and other issues. He made no major blunders while in office. As a result, many Republicans began to consider Bush as a possible presidential candidate for 1996, after only two years in office. What made the possibility enticing was the fact that George W. would face Bill Clinton, the man who had defeated his father in 1992.

Although George W. decided against running in 1996, he remained the Republican favorite for the year 2000. This became especially true after Bush won reelection

As governor of Texas, George W. oversaw more than 130 executions. Cindy Beringer of Austin, Texas, protests against the death penalty by carrying a cardboard cutout of a gun-toting Governor Bush.

Laura and George W. greet the public in an inaugural parade after his second election as governor of Texas. George W. was the first Texas governor to be reelected for a second consecutive term.

in Texas in 1998, becoming the first governor in the history of Texas to win two four-year terms in a row. He had learned how to appeal to both the moderate and the conservative wings of the Republican Party. That same year, his brother Jeb won the Florida race for governor. In George W.'s victory speech, he congratulated Jeb and described himself as a "compassionate conservative"—a term that would serve him well.

Perhaps in preparation for a run at the White House, Bush and his partners decided to sell the Texas Rangers after George W. was reelected. They sold the team in 1998 for $250 million. As his part of the profits, Bush got almost $15 million. He was set financially for life. He could now focus on seeking the Republican nomination for president in 2000, a point not lost on his friends and political advisers. "Congratulations," Bush's friend Joe O'Neill told him after the sale. "You hit the long ball. Now you can run for president. . . . You're free."

When he decided to run for president, George W. knew he would have a long, hard campaign ahead of him.

Chapter **NINE**

THE RACE FOR THE WHITE HOUSE

ALTHOUGH **GEORGE W.** FORMALLY ANNOUNCED HIS intent to run for president in June 1999, his race for the White House actually began the year before. After almost eight years of Bill Clinton's presidency, the Republicans were tired of having a Democrat in the White House.

Although Bush was sure he wanted to *be* president, he wasn't sure if he wanted to *run* for president. Campaigns, especially presidential ones, get personal and nasty. "Bush was genuinely worried about the impact of a presidential campaign on his teenage twins, who feared being made fun of on *Saturday Night Live*," wrote a reporter in *Newsweek* magazine. "And he knew he would miss his comfortable life, jogging, feeding his cats, and . . . bouncing around his new ranch in his Ford Explorer."

In April 1998, Bush attended a private meeting at Stanford University. Leading Republican thinkers, economists, and foreign policy experts wanted to meet Bush to see if he had what it took to be president. They asked him questions about taxes, foreign policy, Social Security, terrorism, and other issues.

Bush was understandably nervous. He realized that in many ways he was auditioning for the group, and his future might well depend on his performance. He broke the ice by making a joke. "You're my professors. I'm the Econ 1 student, and I'm taking it again because I didn't do well in college," he said as the group laughed. After many hours of questioning, Bush passed the test. The group thought he was pleasant, intelligent, and asked good questions. Bush himself seemed surprised at how well the meeting had gone. Leaving the meeting, he joked with one of his advisers that the group "didn't seem to think I was slobbering on my shoes."

Soon prominent Republicans by the dozens made their way to Austin, Texas, to meet Bush. They brought not only their good wishes, but also money and the ability to raise more. By the time Bush officially announced his candidacy, he had attracted more than $15 million to spend on the upcoming primaries. Eventually, he and national Republicans raised more than $350 million for the 2000 presidential election.

Bush and the Republicans believed they would need every penny of it to win. The country was at peace. The economy was going well, and the likely opponent, Vice President Al Gore, had much more government and campaign experience than did Bush. Their only hope seemed to be that Gore would make a huge mistake, which wasn't likely, or that voters would be so disgusted with President Clinton that they would vote against Gore just because of his connection to Clinton.

After Clinton's improper relationship with White House intern Monica Lewinsky had been exposed, he had been impeached for lying under oath about the affair. The president survived the impeachment trial and asked people to forgive him, but he had been

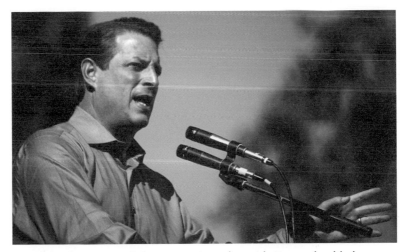

Republicans worried that Vice President Al Gore, the likely Democratic candidate for president, would prove tough to beat.

greatly weakened politically. People seemed to stop taking him seriously. Republicans hated him. And while Democrats defended him, most didn't want to be seen with him. The only one who stood by Clinton publicly was his vice president, Al Gore. The Clinton connection came back to haunt Gore, however, as the relationship between the two became a major campaign issue.

Before Bush could campaign against Gore, he had to win the nomination of his own party. What initially seemed so easy got more difficult when a Republican challenger emerged. Senator John McCain, of Arizona, was a war hero who caught people's attention. During the Vietnam War, McCain had been held prisoner for about five years. He had been tortured so much that he couldn't raise his arms anymore.

McCain looked like a father figure compared with Bush's "frat boy" image. Unlike Bush, who liked to repeat his simple message over and over, McCain liked to deliver his speech and then engage people in spontaneous conversation. In his campaign bus, called the "Straight Talk Express," McCain traveled the country trying to overtake Bush's huge lead and financial advantage. In the first primary, held in New Hampshire on February 1, 2000, Bush lost to McCain.

The New Hampshire defeat took the wind out of Bush's sails. Many of the doubts people had had about Bush began to resurface. The media referred to Bush as "Dubya," a play on both his middle initial and his

Senator John McCain, one of George W.'s leading opponents for the Republican nomination, takes a moment to speak at the Presidential Candidates Youth Forum on January 9, 2000.

Texas drawl. People wondered if George W. had enough political experience, if he was smart enough to campaign against someone as mature as John McCain, and if he would have to call on his father for campaign advice. For a few tense weeks, people wondered if Bush would crack under the pressure, but he remained calm. He didn't fire anybody on his staff. He didn't change his message. He kept his sense of humor. Prior to the New Hampshire defeat, Bush's campaign plane was named *Great Expectations*, reflecting the candidate's optimism. The day after the New Hampshire defeat, Bush greeted reporters as they came aboard the plane. "Welcome to *Expectations*," he told the gathered news media.

After he was named the Republican Party's presidential candidate, George W.'s informal, joking manner often drew negative media attention.

Bolstered by a pep talk from his wife, who urged him to be himself and be more aggressive in fighting for the nomination, Bush headed to South Carolina for the next primary. He defeated McCain in what turned out to be a nasty and controversial primary. By the end of March, Bush was clearly in the lead. The road was now clear for him to be nominated the Republican candidate for president. He accepted the nomination during the Republican National Convention in Philadelphia in July as his teary-eyed parents looked on. Laura Bush confidently gave the opening speech of the convention.

As the campaign got in high gear, George W. faced his harshest criticism. The news media questioned Bush's apparent lack of intelligence, his lack of experience, and his casual attitude. Reporters started writing about how Bush seemed to smirk, as if he was always joking. Another writer who did a profile of Bush even speculated that Bush might be dyslexic or have another learning disability.

Bush denied any problem, but people wondered just how smart he was. Most of all, people wondered whether Bush was mature enough to be president. Not only was Gore extremely intelligent, he was, in some ways, the complete opposite of the fun-loving Bush.

Despite harsh criticism, George W. kept his sense of humor throughout the presidential race.

George W. did not help himself by refusing to talk about what he called his wild youth. At one point he told a reporter he wasn't going to talk about what he'd done thirty years in the past "I famously, and perhaps foolishly, said, 'When I was young and irresponsible, I sometimes behaved young and irresponsibly,'" Bush said. "I thought it was a humorous way to acknowledge that I am not perfect, that as a young man I did some things I am not particularly proud of today. I am still amazed at the rumor mongering set off by that off-hand remark, all apparently spawned by my refusal to itemize a laundry list of things I wish I hadn't done."

Bush countered some of the questions about his sense of judgment by surrounding himself with smart advisers who generally made a good impression when dealing with the public and the press. He also picked Dick Cheney as his choice for vice president. Cheney, a former congressman from Wyoming, had served as the elder Bush's secretary of defense during his presidency.

This selection focused attention on another big issue raised against Bush: how much George W. had benefited from his father's name and accomplishments. "That George W. Bush has traded on his father's name all his life is observably true," said Molly Ivins, a Texas columnist who covered Bush when he was governor of that state. "In fact, one could argue that he's never really done anything else."

As George W.'s running mate, Dick Cheney brought experience and a long political career to the Bush campaign.

George W. responded to these criticisms by saying he was very proud of his father but that he was his own man. He acknowledged he had learned a lot from his father, but it was mainly about how to be a good husband and father. This stance allowed George W. to address one of his main campaign themes, character. The Clinton scandals produced many questions about the president's character. As the spotlight had shifted to Bush and Gore, the two men were forced to demonstrate they had the proper character to be president.

George W.'s ability to relax and laugh was useful during appearances on shows such as Oprah.

Oddly enough, they followed Clinton's lead, even while trying to distance themselves from him. In 1992 candidate Clinton had taken the extraordinary step of going on popular television, visiting the *Arsenio Hall Show* and MTV. To appeal to younger voters, Clinton had played the saxophone and talked about his personal choice of underwear. During the 2000 campaign, Gore and Bush appeared on *Oprah* and *Larry King Live*. In a casual atmosphere, and facing generally friendly questions, Bush and Gore were able to show they were regular guys whom people could trust. "One of the many ironies of the 2000 campaign, conducted in the shadow of Mr. Clinton's tortuous personal and political journey, is that both Mr. Bush and Mr. Gore felt the need to work so hard to humanize themselves, to show that they were regular guys," wrote *New York Times* writer Michiko Kakutani.

Bush also had to guard against doing or saying anything outrageous enough to upset people or further call his qualifications into question. For example, the Bush campaign was accused of subliminally flashing the word *RATS* in a commercial aimed against Democrats. Afterward, Bush was widely ridiculed when he mispronounced the word *subliminal* when responding to criticism of the ad. People laughed at Bush when he called the citizens of Greece "Grecians" instead of Greeks. At one campaign stop, he asked the crowd, who was listening to him talk about education reform, "Is our children learning?" At another campaign stop he was overheard calling a reporter for the *New York Times* a vulgar name. Bush was widely ridiculed for these mishaps. In fact, as the campaign wore on, comedians—from David Letterman and Jay Leno to the players on *Saturday Night Live*—made more and more jokes about the candidates. For the first time in election history, comedians were taken seriously by the candidates and the voters. In fact, people were paying so much attention to the humor that both Bush and Gore found it necessary to go on some of the comedy shows to prove that they could take a joke.

One of the major obstacles that Bush faced was a series of debates held a few weeks before Election Day. Bush's casual attitude and his apparent lack of intellect led some journalists to wonder how well Bush would do against Gore. Gore was considered to be one of the best debaters in the country, a person who could remember facts and was not afraid to attack an

opponent. In the days before the debates, stories cir-
culated predicting that if Bush lost the debates or appeared to be ignorant, he would lose the election.

To the surprise of many, Bush held his own against
Gore. Bush was seen as a nice man who knew
enough. He seemed relaxed, cheerful, friendly, and
hopeful about the future. Bush survived the debates
by sticking to his message, not arguing with Gore, and
constantly repeating the same phrases over and over
again. Once Bush avoided the pitfalls of the debates,
it appeared he stood a good chance of becoming the
next president.

*George W. and Al Gore debate the issues on October 11,
2000, during their second of three televised debates.*

Waiting with his wife and parents for the votes to come in on election night, George W. had no idea he'd have to wait until December to learn whether he had won or lost.

Life—and the election—did not prove to be that easy, however. A few days before the election, the news media reported that as a young man Bush had been arrested for DWI, driving while intoxicated. Bush explained that he had not said anything about the arrest because he did not want his daughters to know about it. That in turn started questions about whether he had ever used drugs.

The drunken driving controversy faded, however, in comparison to the uproar on election night. The vote for president proved to be one of the most controversial in United States history. It was not settled until thirty-five days after the November 7 vote.

ELECTORAL COLLEGE

Although people in the United States think they are directly electing the president when they vote, they are not. People are actually voting for the electors who will later vote for president. Sound confusing? It can be, but blame the confusion on the Founding Fathers, who wisely created something called the electoral college. Members of the electoral college decide who becomes president of the United States.

Many people who vote probably aren't even aware of the electoral college. That's because members of the electoral college usually do their job routinely and without controversy. But sometimes controversy erupts, and people question what the electoral college is and why it has so much power. The electoral college is a group of people who gather once every four years in late December to elect the president. That is why they are called electors.

The electoral college was created in 1787 during the Constitutional Convention in Philadelphia because the Founding Fathers could not agree on the best way to elect a president. Some wanted a popular vote while others favored having Congress select from among the candidates. The electoral college was seen as the best compromise.

How are the electors selected? Indirectly, by the voters. Each state has a specific number of electors, or electoral votes, equal to the size of its congressional delegation: its two senators plus its members of the House of Representatives. The number of electoral votes ranges from three in tiny Rhode Island and the District of Columbia to fifty-four in California. Each state's electoral votes usually go in a winner-take-all format to whichever presidential candidate gets the most votes from registered voters in that state. This means that if a candidate loses in large states, even by one vote, he (or she) does not get any electoral votes from those states. If a candidate loses enough big states, he would not get enough electoral votes to win—even with all the electoral votes of the smaller states. That is why a candidate can lose the popular vote but still win the electoral vote and become president. That is what happened in the 2000 election between George W. Bush and Al Gore. Gore won the popular vote 50,996,116 to 50,456,169; Bush won the electoral college 271 to 266, with one voter casting a blank ballot. It was the fifth time in U.S. history that a candidate won the popular vote but lost the presidency.

Electors, however, are free to vote for whomever they want. Although there are some state penalties for being what is called an unfaithful elector, there is no federal law or anything in the Constitution that requires electors to vote for the candidate that won their state. Such switching has happened only about nine times. Most people don't switch because they are loyal to their party and its candidate. Only electors of the state's winning party vote in the electoral college. Switching votes, however, was a big concern of the Bush camp in the 2000 election. Not only was the electoral vote close, which meant every vote was crucial, but Gore had won the popular vote. Bush supporters were worried that some electors might have thought this situation was unfair and vote for Gore. That did not happen, however, and Bush won the vote of the electoral college.

Over the years there have been more than seven hundred attempts to abolish or reform the electoral college, but the smaller states have been able to defeat these proposals. If candidates had to win only the popular vote, they would spend all their time campaigning in cities and states with the highest populations. They could then ignore smaller states, such as Rhode Island or North Dakota, because there would not be enough voters in those states to justify the amount of time spent campaigning in them. The electoral college system at least ensures that the voices of the smaller states are heard.

The controversy centered on the state of Florida, where George W.'s younger brother Jeb was the governor. Problems with counting the votes delayed a final decision on election night. At first the media declared that Gore had won the state. Then it appeared that George W. had won. Whoever won Florida's twenty-five electoral votes would win the election. In the days that followed, both parties went to court. The Florida Supreme Court wanted a recount in questionable counties, which probably would have favored Gore. On December 12, the U.S. Supreme Court ordered the counting to stop, with Bush ahead by a few hundred votes. George W. Bush had finally secured his place in history. He would be the forty-third president of the United States.

Jeb Bush, right, *governor of Florida, shares a lighthearted moment with his father and brother as election uncertainty drags on.*

Voters show their support for George W. during the long recounting process. One dedicated participant is dressed as a "chad," the part of Florida ballots that is punched out to indicate a vote. Chads that were not completely punched out caused some of the postelection confusion about the outcome.

But even after Bush was declared the winner, the threat still existed that his victory would be challenged in Congress or that one or more of the electors in the electoral college would switch camps and vote for Gore. The tense situation finally calmed down when Gore went on national television and said Bush would be the next president. In a short speech, Gore asked that people support the new president. In response, Bush promised to be president to everyone in the United States and to unite what had become a deeply divided country.

After a long and difficult wait to see if he had won the election, George W. takes the oath of office to become the forty-third U.S. president.

CONCLUSION

As a freezing rain fell on Washington, D.C., George W. Bush was sworn in as the forty-third president of the United States on January 20, 2001. The inauguration officially ended all doubt about the outcome of the presidential election, but the unusual circumstances of the election left a cloud hanging over Bush's victory.

As he stood on the steps of the Capitol, George W. Bush was well aware that he had history working against him. The four other men (Thomas Jefferson, John Quincy Adams, Rutherford B. Hayes, and Grover Cleveland) who had become president after such controversial elections had all faced trouble getting people to rally around them. Until George W. was elected, John Quincy Adams had been the only son of a United States president also to be elected president.

Aware of this, and perhaps trying to lighten his son's heart, George W.'s father began calling his son Quincy shortly after the younger Bush was named president-elect. The joking continued even through the inauguration.

But, as *Newsweek* magazine pointed out, "If you're Dubya, it may not be that funny; the younger Adams only served one term."

Apart from history, Bush also had to deal with the anger generated by his election victory. During the campaign Bush had promised the country that he would be a uniter and not a divider. After Bush took the oath of office from Chief Justice William Rehnquist, he had to make good on that promise by giving the most important speech of his life.

To prepare, Bush spent five weeks reading the inauguration speeches of former presidents. He knew that "he must use this speech to wipe away, like spilled milk, the questions of the legitimacy arising from his strange path to the Oval Office."

Unification was, indeed, the main theme of George W.'s inauguration speech. As millions watched on television and hundreds of friends and family stood nearby, Bush made a solemn pledge to "work to build a single nation of justice and opportunity. I know this is within our reach." Bush also promised to restore civility, respect, and responsibility to the presidency while creating what he called a compassionate country and government. After Bush finished his speech, supporters gathered on the Capitol steps cheered as a band began playing the traditional song reserved for only the president of the United States, "Hail to the Chief."

Even as the music was playing, however, thousands of protesters chanted and yelled in the streets of Washington, D.C. The demonstrations were the first major protests on inauguration day since 1973, when Richard Nixon was sworn in while tens of thousands protested the Vietnam War. The anti-Bush demonstrators, while fewer in number, still required the tightest security ever for a presidential inauguration. Police

George W.'s inauguration did not bring an end to protests and demonstrations. Many people remained skeptical about the election results in Florida and the Supreme Court's decision to declare George W. president.

officers stood every few feet along the inauguration parade route as protesters voiced displeasure not only about Bush's stand on civil rights and abortion, but also about the fact that he had been *selected* (by the Supreme Court) and not *elected* to the presidency. One sign held aloft in the crowd during the televised inaugural parade seemed to sum up their feelings. It proclaimed, "Hail to the Thief!"

"The people of America were robbed of their choice," said one demonstrator, a bus driver from the state of Washington. Comedian Dick Gregory accused Bush of stealing the election. "If you stole my car," he told the crowd, "I'm never going to accept that it's your car."

As president, George W. faces the challenge of proving that his administration will work in the interest of all people of the United States.

The controversy over the election hurt Bush in a couple of ways. It focused attention away from George W.'s remarkable transformation from being an irresponsible youth to being the most powerful man in the world. Also, instead of focusing all of his attention on delivering his campaign promises of cutting taxes and improving the education system, Bush knew he would have to expend a lot of energy to convince people that he is the true president of the United States.

"Expectations in this country [are] we can't get anything done," Bush said at a luncheon with congressional leaders on Inauguration Day. "People say, 'Well, gosh, the election was so close, nothing will happen except finger-pointing and name-calling and bitterness.' I'm here to tell the country that things will get done, that we're going to rise above expectations, that both Republicans and Democrats will come together to do what's right for America."

With those words, George W. began his adventure as president of the United States. He was the first president elected in the new millennium, and it seemed fitting because of the historic nature of his election and the great debates that it inspired.

DEFINING A PRESIDENCY: AMERICA IN CRISIS

O n September 11, 2001, less than a year into President George W. Bush's term in office, tragedy struck the United States. Hijacked U.S. passenger planes crashed into the towers of the World Trade Center in New York City and the Pentagon in Washington, D.C. The targets were prime symbols of U.S. economic and military might. A fourth hijacked passenger plane failed to reach its target but crashed into the Pennsylvania countryside southeast of Pittsburgh.

The events of September 11, a day that will forever be infamous in U.S. history, unfolded like a bad dream. At approximately 8:45 A.M., American Airlines Flight 11, carrying ninety-two people, crashed into the north tower of the World Trade Center. About eighteen minutes later, United Airlines Flight 175 smashed into the south tower of the World Trade Center with sixty-five people aboard. At roughly 9:40 A.M., American Airlines Flight 77, originally bound for Los Angeles with sixty-four people aboard, plowed into the Pentagon. United Airlines Flight 93 crashed in Pennsylvania at about 10:00 A.M., killing forty-five people. Later that morning, both towers of the World Trade Center collapsed, taking thousands more innocent lives.

President Bush, speaking from a Florida elementary school, addressed the nation minutes after the attacks on the World Trade Center:

> Today we've had a national tragedy. Two airplanes have crashed into the World Trade Center in an apparent terrorist attack on our country. I have spoken to the vice president, to the governor of New York, to the director of the FBI, and I've ordered that the full resources of the federal government go to help the victims and their families and to conduct a full-scale investigation to hunt down and to find those folks who committed this act.

Before the events of September 11, the focus of the Bush administration had been on education and the economy. After the collapse of both towers of the World Trade Center, the focus shifted to a war on terrorism. This catastrophe was not only the defining moment of Bush's presidency but also a defining moment in the history of the United States. Speaking from the Oval Office the night of the attacks, President Bush attempted to encourage a distraught American public: "These acts shattered steel, but they cannot dent the steel of American resolve."

George Bush greets firefighters and rescue workers at the damaged Pentagon the day after terrorists crashed a hijacked passenger plane into the headquarters of the U.S. Department of Defense.

SOURCES

14 J. H. Hatfield, *Fortunate Son: George W. Bush and the Making of an American President* (New York: Soft Skull Press, 2000), 5.

18 George W. Bush, *A Charge to Keep* (New York: William Morrow and Company, Inc., 1999), 18.

18 George Lardner Jr. and Lois Romano "Tragedy Created Bush Mother-Son Bond," *Washington Post*, July 26, 1999, A-1.

19 "Tragedy Created Bush Mother-Son Bond," A-1.

19 Bush, 14.

20 "Tragedy Created Bush Mother-Son Bond," A-1.

20 Elizabeth Mitchell, *W: Revenge of the Bush Dynasty* (New York: Hyperion, 2000), 34.

20–21 Ibid.

21 "Tragedy Created Bush Mother-Son Bond," A-1.

24 Bush, 19.

24 Ibid.

25 Mitchell, 15.

26 George Lardner Jr. and Lois Romano, "Bush: So-So Student but a Campus Mover," *Washington Post*, July 27, 1999, A-1.

26 Ibid.

29 Bush, 46.

30 "In His Own Words: 'Leadership Comes in All Forms,'" *Washington Post*, July 27, 1999, A-11.

30 "Bush: So-So Student," A-1.

30 "In His Own Words," A-11.

31 Ibid.

32–33 Bush, 47.

33 Bush, 47.

33 "Bush: So-So Student," A-1.

36 Bush, 48.

36 Ibid., 50.

36–37 Ibid.

40 Mitchell, 106.

40 Bush, 50.

40–41 Ibid., 50–51.

48–49 George Lardner Jr. and Lois Romano, "At Height of Vietnam, Bush Picks Guard," *Washington Post*, July 28, 1999, A-1.

49 Ibid.

50 Bush, 59.

50 Ibid., 58.

50 51 Ibid., 59.

51 Ibid., 58.

54–55 Ibid., 79.

60 George Lardner Jr. and Lois Romano, "Bush Name Helps Fuel Oil Dealings," *Washington Post*, July 30, 1999, A-1.

60 Daniel Cohen, *George W. Bush: The Family Business* (Brookfield, CT: The Millbrook Press, 2000), 25.

65 Bush, 132–33.

66 Hatfield, 123–24.

74 Cohen, 30.

74 Hatfield, 124.

75 George Lardner Jr. and Lois Romano, "Bush's Move up to the Majors," *Washington Post*, July 31, 1999, A-1.

77 Ibid.

79–80 Evan Thomas et al., "The Favorite Son: Pumping Iron, Digging Gold, Pressing Flesh," *Newsweek*, November 20, 2000, 52.

80 Ibid., 51.

80 Ibid.

83 Ibid.

85–86 Bush, 133.

87 Molly Ivins and Lou Dubose, *Shrub: The Short but Happy Political Life of George W. Bush* (New York: Random House, 2000), xix.

87–88 Michiko Kakutani, "An Essay: With the Guy Next Door in the Oval Office, the Presidency Shrinks Further," *New York Times*, January 19, 2001, <http://www.nytimes.com> (January 26, 2001).

88 Thomas, 57.

97 Howard Fineman and Martha Brant, "The Test of His Life," *Newsweek,* December 25, 2000/January 1, 2001, 33.

98 David E. Sanger, "Momentous Challenges as Bush Reaches for 12 Minutes of Inaugural Fame," *New York Times,* n.d., <http://www.nytimes.com> (January 20, 2001).

98 Melinda Henneberger, "The Inauguration: The Speech; In His Address, Bush Lingers on a Promise to Care," *New York Times,* January 21, 2001, 13.

99 David E. Rosenbaum, "The Inauguration: The Demonstrations; Protesters in the Thousands Sound Off in the Capital," *New York Times,* January 21, 2001, 15.

101 Nick Anderson, James Gerstenzang, and Doyle McManus, "Bush Vows to Bring Nation Together," *Los Angeles Times,* January 21, 2001, <http://www.latimes.com> (n.d.).

102 "Thousands Feared Killed in Terrorist Strike that Crumbles World Trade Centers, Shuts Government," *Startribune.com,* September 12, 2001. <http://www.startribune.com/stories/484/685219.html> (September 17, 2001).

102 "Chronology of Events," *Startribune.com,* September 12, 2001, <http://www.startribune.com/stories/1576/686283.html> (September 17, 2001).

102 "A Carefully Planned, Precisely Coordinated Attack," *Startribune.com,* September 13, 2001. <http://www.startribune.com/stories/484/687906.html> (September 17, 2001).

103 "Bush Condemns Attacks, Vows to 'find those responsible,'" *Startribune.com,* September 12, 2001. <http://www.startribune.com/stories/484/685011.html> (September 17, 2001).

BIBLIOGRAPHY

Anderson, Nick, James Gerstenzang, and Doyle McManus. "Bush Vows to Bring Nation Together." *Los Angeles Times,* January 21, 2001, <http://www.latimes.com> (n.d.).

Bush, George W. *A Charge to Keep.* New York: William Morrow and Company, Inc., 1999.

Cohen, Daniel. *George W. Bush: The Family Business.* Brookfield, CT: The Millbrook Press, 2000.

Fineman, Howard, and Martha Brant. "The Test of His Life." *Newsweek,* December 25, 2000/January 1, 2001.

Hatfield, J. H. *Fortunate Son: George W. Bush and the Making of an American President.* New York: Soft Skull Press, 2000.

Ivins, Molly, and Lou Dubose. *Shrub: The Short but Happy Political Life of George W. Bush.* New York: Random House, 2000.

Kakutani, Michiko, "An Essay: With the Guy Next Door in the Oval Office, the Presidency Shrinks Further." *New York Times,* January 19, 2001, <http://www.nytimes.com> (January 26, 2001).

Mitchell, Elizabeth. *W: Revenge of the Bush Dynasty.* New York: Hyperion, 2000.

Sanger, David E. "Momentous Challenges as Bush Reaches for 12 Minutes of Inaugural Fame." *New York Times,* n.d. <http://www.nytimes.com> (January 20, 2001).

Sheehy, Gail. "The Accidental Candidate." *Vanity Fair,* October 2000.

Thomas, Evan, et al. "The Favorite Son: Pumping Iron, Digging Gold, Pressing Flesh." *Newsweek,* November 20, 2000.

FOR FURTHER READING

Bush, Barbara. *Barbara Bush: A Memoir.* New York: Scribner's, 1994.

Bush, George H. W. *All the Best, George Bush: My Life in Letters and Other Writings.* New York: Scribner's, 1999.

Bush, George W. *A Charge to Keep.* New York: William Morrow and Company, Inc., 1999.

Dershowitz, Alan M. *Supreme Injustice: How the High Court Hijacked Election 2000.* New York: Oxford University Press, 2001.

Gormley, Beatrice. *President George W. Bush: Our Forty-Third President.* New York: Aladdin Paperbacks, 2001.

Marsh, Carole, and Kathy Zimmer. *George W. Bush: America's Newest President, and His White House Family.* The Here & Now Series. Peachtree City, GA: Gallopade International, 2001.

Minutaglio, Bill. *First Son: George W. Bush and the Bush Family Dynasty.* New York: Random House, 1999.

Parnet, Herbert. *George Bush: The Life of a Lone Star Yankee.* New York: Scribner's, 1997.

Posner, Richard A. *Breaking the Deadlock: The 2000 Election, the Constitution, and the Courts.* Princeton, NJ: Princeton University Press, 2001.

Russell, Jon, ed. *The Complete Book of Inaugural Addresses of the Presidents of the United States: From George Washington to George W. Bush 1789 to 2001.* Seattle: iUniverse Online Books, 2001.

INDEX

OTHER TITLES FROM LERNER AND A&E®:

Arthur Ashe
The Beatles
Benjamin Franklin
Bill Gates
Bruce Lee
Carl Sagan
Chief Crazy Horse
Christopher Reeve
Edgar Allan Poe
Eleanor Roosevelt
George Lucas
Gloria Estefan
Jack London
Jacques Cousteau
Jane Austen
Jesse Owens
Jesse Ventura
Jimi Hendrix
John Glenn
Latin Sensations
Legends of Dracula

Legends of Santa Claus
Louisa May Alcott
Madeleine Albright
Malcom X
Mark Twain
Maya Angelou
Mohandas Gandhi
Mother Teresa
Nelson Mandela
Oprah Winfrey
Princess Diana
Queen Cleopatra
Queen Latifah
Rosie O'Donnell
Saint Joan of Arc
Thurgood Marshall
William Shakespeare
Wilma Rudolph
Women in Space
Women of the Wild West

ABOUT THE AUTHOR

Herón Márquez, born in Mexico, moved to California at the age of six. After a short career playing semiprofessional baseball, he took up writing. He has worked as a journalist for such papers as the *Albuquerque Journal, New York Daily News, Los Angeles Times, Santa Barbara News Press,* and the *Minneapolis Star Tribune.* Márquez lives in St. Paul, Minnesota, with his wife Traecy.

PHOTO ACKNOWLEDGMENTS

Photographs used with the permission of: © Rommel Pecson, pp. 2, 6; © AFP/CORBIS, pp. 10, 41, 76, 87, 90; George Bush Presidential Library, pp. 12, 14, 15, 17, 19, 21, 28, 38, 44, 55, 56, 59, 64, 71; Classmates.com Yearbook Archives, pp. 22, 26, 27; © Bettmann/CORBIS, pp. 31, 42, 46, 57, 58, 62, 66, 68; © Rykoff Collection/CORBIS, p. 35; The *Toronto Sun,* p. 49; © Wally McNamee/CORBIS, p. 52; Carol T. Powers, The White House, p. 70; David Woo/The *Dallas Morning News,* p. 72; Richard Michael Pruitt/The *Dallas Morning News,* p. 74; AP/Wide World Photos, pp. 77, 88, 96, 100; © Jana Birchman, p. 78; © Joseph Sohm; ChromoSohm Inc./CORBIS, pp. 81, 83; © Reuters NewMedia Inc./CORBIS pp. 84, 91, 94, 95, 99; © Donna Binder, p. 85; © AFP/CORBIS, p. 103.

Hardcover: front, © Reuters NewMedia Inc./CORBIS; back, George Bush Presidential Library.
Soft cover: front, © Reuters NewMedia Inc./CORBIS; back, © Reuters NewMedia Inc./CORBIS.